Pupil Book 3
Comprehension

Author: Abigail Steel

William Collins' dream of knowledge for all began with the publication of his first book in 1819. A self-educated mill worker, he not only enriched millions of lives, but also founded a flourishing publishing house. Today, staying true to this spirit, Collins books are packed with inspiration, innovation and practical expertise. They place you at the centre of a world of possibility and give you exactly what you need to explore it.

Collins. Freedom to teach.

Published by Collins
An imprint of HarperCollins*Publishers*
The News Building
1 London Bridge Street
London
SE1 9GF

Browse the complete Collins catalogue at
www.collins.co.uk

British Library Cataloguing in Publication Data
A Catalogue record for this publication is available from the British Library

Publishing Manager: Tom Guy
Project Managers: Dawn Booth and Kate Ellis
Editor: Hannah Hirst-Dunton
Cover design and artwork: Amparo Barrera
Internal design concept: Amparo Barrera
Typesetting: Jouve India Private Ltd
Illustrations: Dante Ginevra, Adrian Bijloo, Aptara and QBS

Printed in Italy by Grafica Veneta S.p.A.

Acknowledgements

The publishers wish to thank the following for permission to reproduce content. Every effort has been made to trace copyright holders and to obtain their permission for the use of copyright materials. The publishers will gladly receive any information enabling them to rectify any error or omission at the first opportunity.

The Estate of Val Biro for an extract from *Gumdrop has a Birthday* by Val Biro, Puffin, 1992, copyright © Val Biro; John Talbot for an extract and 3 images from *The Dragon's Cold* by John Talbot, text © 1986 John Talbot. Reproduced by permission of John Talbot; Egmont UK Ltd for an extract from *The Owl Who Was Afraid of the Dark* by Jill Tomlinson. Text copyright © The Estate of Jill Tomlinson 1968. Published by Egmont UK Ltd London and used with permission; Penguin Random House for an extract and 2 illustrations from *The Tale of Peter Rabbit* by Beatrix Potter, copyright © Frederick Warne & Co., 1902, 2002. Reproduced by permission of Frederick Warne & Co. www.peterrabbit.com; and Faber & Faber Ltd and HarperCollins Publishers for an extract from 'Roger the Dog' by Ted Hughes, from *Collected Poems for Children* by Ted Hughes and *What is the Truth? A Farmyard Fable for the Young* by Ted Hughes, copyright © Ted Hughes, 1984, Faber and Faber Ltd. Reproduced by permission of Faber & Faber Ltd and HarperCollins Publishers.

(t = top, c = centre, b = bottom)

p. 28 (t) successo images/Shutterstock, p. 28 Henrik Larsson/Shutterstock, p. 29 cbstockphoto/Alamy, p. 30 InsectWorld/Shutterstock, p. 46 (t) Gregory Dimijian/Science Photo Library, p. 46 (b) Jan-Nor Photography/Shutterstock, p. 47 (t) Dirk Ercken/Shutterstock, p. 47 (b) Matteo Sani/Shutterstock, p. 48 Arco Images GmbH/Alamy

Pupil Book 3

Comprehension

Contents

Fiction: 'Gumdrop has a Birthday'

From 'Gumdrop Has a Birthday' by Val Biro

Mr Oldcastle invited several of his friends to help celebrate Gumdrop's birthday. After they gave Gumdrop his presents …

The guests gathered round Gumdrop to wish him Many Happy Returns and another fifty years of happy motoring.

"For he's a jolly good fellow," they sang, and "Happy birthday, dear Gumdrop, happy birthday to you!"

Mr Oldcastle was very happy and he thanked them all for Gumdrop's sake.

"And here is the birthday cake!" he said. But it wasn't on the table – and it hadn't rolled away. It had vanished!

"Who took the cake!" he cried.

Horace was very happy too. He sat on the ground and he looked very fat. There wasn't a crumb to be seen, because he likes cakes.

Get started

Copy these sentences carefully and complete them by filling in the gaps.

1. It was Gumdrop's _____.

2. _____ invited several friends to celebrate.

3. The guests wished Gumdrop Many Happy _____.

4. "For he's a jolly _____ fellow," they sang!

5. Horace sat on the ground and he looked very _____.

Try these

Write a sentence to answer each question. One has been done for you.

1. What did the guests do before they sang to Gumdrop?

   Answer: *Before the guests sang to Gumdrop, they wished him Many Happy Returns.*

2. How did Mr Oldcastle feel when the guests were singing?

3. Why did he feel like this?

4. What had happened to the cake?

5. Do you think Mr Oldcastle wanted this to happen? Why do you think this?

Now try these

1. How might Mr Oldcastle feel now? What might he do next? Write one or two sentences as though Mr Oldcastle is saying them.

2. Think about the presents Gumdrop may have been given. Write about Mr Oldcastle opening the presents for Gumdrop and how he felt while he did it.

3. Draw a picture of the birthday party. Use the text to give you ideas.

Poetry: 'Caterpillars'

From 'Caterpillars' by Eric Slater

Wiggling, woggling up and down
Painted as bright as a circus clown
Clinging to twigs with tiny feet
Always looking for something to eat.
Some have bristles, some have spots
Some have patches like polka dots
They're brown and yellow, green and blue
But mostly green like the leaves they chew.

Get started

Copy these lines carefully and complete them by filling in the gaps.

1. Some have patches like _____
_____

2. Clinging to twigs with _____ feet

3. But mostly green like the leaves they
_____.

4. Wiggling, woggling _____ _____
_____

5. _____ looking for something to eat.

Try these

Write a sentence to answer each question. One has been done for you.

1. According to the poem, are all caterpillars green?

   Answer: *According to the poem, not all caterpillars are green. They can also be brown, yellow or blue.*

2. What are 'bristles'? Use a dictionary for help if necessary.

3. Are the caterpillars really painted?

4. Why do you think the poet says that they are painted?

5. In your own words, explain what you think the poet means by 'woggling'.

Now try these

1. The words 'like a circus clown' compare the caterpillars to a clown. What else could the caterpillars be like? Write down at least three ideas.

2. Find the four pairs of words in the poem that rhyme. Then write two new pairs of rhyming lines about the caterpillars.

3. Draw a picture of the caterpillars described in the poem.

Poetry: 'The Cow'

The friendly cow all red and white,
I love with all my heart:
She gives me cream with all her might,
To eat with apple-tart.
She wanders lowing here and there.
And yet she cannot stray,
All in the pleasant open air,
The pleasant light of day:
And blown by all the winds that pass
And wet with all the showers,
She walks among the meadow grass
And eats the meadow flowers.

Robert Louis Stevenson

Get started

Copy these lines carefully and complete them by filling in the gaps.

1. She wanders _____ here and there.

2. And blown by all the _____

3. And yet she _____ stray,

4. I _____ with all my heart:

5. The _____ light of day:

Try these

Write a sentence to answer each question. One has been done for you.

1. What is this poem about?

   Answer: *This poem is about a cow.*

2. Why does the poet love the cow?

3. What does the word 'lowing' mean? Use a dictionary for help if necessary.

4. What does 'with all her might' mean?

5. When does the cow go into her shed?

Now try these

1. Do you think the cow enjoys her life in the field? Make some notes about what the poem says to explain why you think this.

2. Imagine the cow can write a reply. Write four lines from the cow's point of view.

3. Use the information in the poem to draw a picture of the cow.

Non-fiction (news report): Monkey Business

LATEST NEWS

Cheeky chimps on the motorway

Drivers were surprised to see monkeys running all over the road yesterday. The lorry taking them to their new home at Burwell Zoo had broken down. While the lorry driver went to get help, one of the monkeys managed to lift the latch on the door. Inspector Baker said the monkeys looked like they were having great fun.

They climbed all over the road signs and scrambled up the lamp posts. One even sat on top of the police car! Some

drivers got irate because of the traffic jam, but most drivers were prepared to see the funny side. "I'm pleased to say all the cheeky chimps are now safely back in the zoo," said Inspector Baker last night.

Get started

Copy these sentences carefully and complete them by filling in the gaps.

1. Drivers were _____ to see monkeys running all over the road yesterday.

2. The lorry taking them to their new home at _____ Zoo had broken down.

3. One of the monkeys _____ to lift the latch on the door.

4. The monkeys looked like they were having _____ fun.

5. One even sat on top of the _____ car!

Try these

Write a sentence to answer each question. One has been done for you.

1. Where had the lorry been going?

   Answer: *The lorry had been going to Burwell Zoo.*

2. What happened in the end?

3. In your own words, explain how the car drivers felt about the monkeys' escape. Use a dictionary for help if necessary.

4. Do you think Inspector Baker was angry about the monkeys' escape? Why do you think this?

5. How do you think the lorry driver felt?

Now try these

1. Why might people want to read this news report?

2. Imagine the news reporter interviewed one of the drivers. Write at least three sentences as though a driver is saying them.

3. Draw a picture of Inspector Baker and the lorry driver. Show how you think they may be feeling.

Fiction (traditional story): 'Thunder and Lightning'

'Thunder and Lightning' – a Nigerian folk story

Thunder and Lightning were two grumpy old sheep.
Lightning would lose his temper and knock down trees and burn the crops. Thunder, his mother, who had an extremely loud voice, would shout at him.

The villagers became really fed up with them. The villagers kept complaining about the damage – and the noise!

In the end, the village chief said he couldn't stand it any longer. He said they would have to go far away. He sent them to live in the sky!

But things didn't work out as the chief intended. To this day, Lightning still enjoys getting his own back on the villagers, and Thunder still shouts at the top of her voice and keeps the villagers awake at night.

Get started

Copy these sentences carefully and complete them by filling in the gaps using words from the text.

1. _____ and _____ were two grumpy old sheep.

2. Thunder had an extremely _____ voice.

3. The villagers complained about the _____ and the _____.

4. The village chief sent the sheep to live in the _____.

5. Thunder still keeps the _____ awake at night.

Try these

Write a sentence to answer each question. One has been done for you.

1. What did Lightning do to annoy everyone in the story?

   Answer: *Lightning lost his temper, knocked down trees and burnt crops.*

2. What is lightning in real life? What damage can it do? Use a dictionary for help if necessary.

3. How did the villagers feel before the chief sent the sheep away?

4. What do you think they wanted to happen?

5. Do you think they were happy in the end? Why do you think this?

Now try these

1. How may the villagers feel now? Write one or two sentences as though a villager is saying them.

2. Rewrite the story from the village chief's perspective. Think about what he wants and how he feels.

3. Draw a picture of Thunder and Lightning bothering the villagers.

Fiction (fable): 'The Lion and the Mouse'

'The Lion and the Mouse' – a fable by Aesop

One day, a mouse happened to run over the paws of a sleeping lion. Angrily, the mighty beast woke. He was about to crush the little animal when the mouse cried out, "Please, mighty king of all the animals, spare me. I would be only a tiny mouthful, and I'm sure you would not like the taste. Besides, I might be able to help you someday. You never can tell."

The idea that this tiny creature could ever help him amused the lion so much that he let his little prisoner go.

Some time after this, the lion was roaming in the forest and looking for food. Suddenly he was caught in a hunter's net. The more the lion struggled, the more stuck he became; his roar of rage echoed through the forest. Hearing the sound, the mouse ran to the trap and began to gnaw the ropes that bound the lion. It was not long before he had bitten through the last cord with his little teeth and set the huge beast free.

Moral: Don't belittle little things.

Get started

Copy these sentences carefully and complete them by filling in the gaps using words from the text.

1. A mouse happened to run over the _____ of a sleeping lion.

2. He was about to _____ the little animal.

3. "Please, mighty _____ of all the animals, spare me."

4. The idea that this tiny creature could ever help him _____ the lion.

5. The mouse ran to the _____ and began to gnaw the ropes that bound the lion.

Try these

Write a sentence to answer each question. One has been done for you.

1. Who are the characters in this story?

   Answer: *The characters in the story are a lion and a mouse.*

2. How did the mouse save the lion?

3. In your own words, explain the moral of the story.

4. Why do you think the mouse saved the lion?

5. Do you think the lion expected the mouse to ever help him? Why do you think this?

Now try these

1. How might the lion feel now? Write one or two sentences as though the lion is saying them.

2. Write at least six lines of dialogue that may have occurred between the lion and the mouse after the story.

3. Draw a picture of the mouse rescuing the lion.

Fiction: 'The Dragon's Cold'

From 'The Dragon's Cold' by John Talbot

"Look at this," said Mimi. "Look what I've found!"

"It's very long," said Alex.

"And it's incredibly heavy," said Roland.

"What can it be?" asked Spike.

"It's a dragon!" they all shouted.

"Let's get out of here!"

"Oh, don't go," said the dragon. "I won't hurt you." He sounded very sad.

"What's the matter?" asked Mimi.

"It's this dreadful cold," sniffed the dragon. "It's completely put my fire out. All my family and friends sent me away. 'Duncan,' they said, 'no one wants a dragon without fire.'"

"We want you," said Mimi, "and we'll take care of you."

"We'll think of something," agreed Alex.

Get started

Copy these sentences carefully and complete them by filling in the gaps using words from the poem.

    1. "Look at this," said _____.

    2. "Let's get _____ of here!"

    3. "Oh, don't go," said the dragon. "I won't _____ you."

    4. It's _____ put my fire out.

    5. "We'll think of _____."

Try these

Write a sentence to answer each question. One has been done for you.

    1. Who are the characters in this story?

       Answer: *The characters in the story are Mimi, Alex, Roland, Spike and the dragon.*

    2. Who or what is Duncan?

    3. How does Duncan feel? Why does he feel like that?

    4. When the children first find the dragon, how do they feel? How do you know?

    5. At the end of the extract, how do the children feel? How do you know?

Now try these

1. How might Duncan feel now? What may he want to do next? Write one or two sentences as though Duncan is saying them.

2. Imagine you are with the children in the story. Write a more powerful description of stumbling across the dragon. What does he look like? Smell like? Sound like? How would you feel? What would you say?

3. Draw a detailed picture of Duncan being discovered. Use the text to give you ideas.

Non-fiction (letter): Gran's New House

'Seaview'
Cliff Lane
Sandy Bay
SY13 7AB
Saturday 6th May

Dear Annie, Tim and Jenny,

We moved into our new house just three days ago. I think we are going to like it, even though it is strange not living in the same town as you any more. From our front windows we can see the sea, and at the back we have lovely views of the hills.

The removal truck broke down so it took six hours to get here, when it should have only taken about two hours!

Grandad and I thought you may like to come and stay for a few days in the school holiday. If Mum and Dad can't come, then we'll meet you at the station.

With much love,
Gran xxx

Get started

Copy these sentences carefully and complete them by filling in the gaps using words from the letter.

1. We moved into our new house just _____ days ago.

2. From our _____ windows we can see the sea.

3. At the back we have lovely _____ of the hills.

4. The journey should have only taken about _____ hours!

5. I thought you may like to come and _____ for a few days.

Try these

Write a sentence to answer each question. One has been done for you.

1. To whom was the letter written?

   Answer: *The letter was written to Annie, Tim and Jenny.*

2. What are the best things about the new house?

3. Why does Gran think it feels strange living at the new house?

4. Who lives with Gran?

5. Do you think Gran is glad they moved? Why do you think this?

Now try these

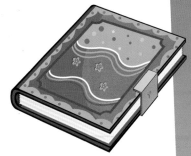

1. How might the children feel about Gran moving house? Write one or two sentences as though one of the children is writing them.

2. Write a short diary entry as though one of the children is writing it. Explain in more detail how this child feels about the move, and whether they want to go and visit Gran.

3. Draw a detailed picture of Gran's new house. Use the text to give you ideas.

Non-fiction (information text): Ants

Ants' nest

Tiny tunnels lead into the nest.

Each nest is a mass of tunnels and rooms.

Types of ant

In every nest there are three types of ant.

The biggest are the queen ants. Queen ants have wings.

The big males aren't quite as big as a queen, but they do have wings.

The small ants are the worker ants, and they don't have wings.

Who does what?

A queen ant lives in one room of the nest. She stays in her room all the time and lays hundreds of eggs.

The big male ants mate with a queen, and then die.

The worker ants collect the food. They feed the young ants, keep the nest clean and dig more rooms and tunnels as they are needed. They also keep away ants from other nests.

Get started

Copy these sentences from the text carefully and complete them by filling in the gaps.

1. Tiny _____ lead into the nest.

2. Each nest is a mass of tunnels and _____.

3. In every nest there are _____ types of ant.

4. Queen ants have _____.

5. The _____ _____ ants are the worker ants.

Try these

Write a sentence to answer each question. One has been done for you.

1. How many rooms does the queen ant live in?

Answer: *The queen ant lives in one room.*

2. Which ants do the most different kinds of jobs?

3. Do big male ants collect food?

4. Which ants have wings?

5. Which type of ant digs the queen ant's room?

Now try these

1. In your own words, write three interesting facts about ants.

2. Draw a picture of a queen ant and label it, using the details given in the extract.

3. Draw a diagram of an ants' nest and label it, using the details given in the extract. Add examples of each type of ant, where you think they would be in the nest.

Non-fiction (information text): On Holiday

Jo's family is on holiday.

They are given instructions and a map at their campsite.

SANDY BAY HOLIDAY PARK

Welcome to Sandy Bay Holiday Park. We hope you will enjoy your stay with us.

To help you find your feet as quickly as possible, may we offer some advice.

1. Walk around the park to get your bearings.

2. Visit our supermarket to stock up with provisions.

3. Drop in to the information centre to pick up some leaflets about local attractions.

We don't have many rules, but those we do have are to ensure you and other guests enjoy a relaxed holiday, away from the hurly-burly of everyday life!

Rule 1: Please return to the park no later than 11.30 pm.

Rule 2: No noise outside your caravan or tent after midnight.

Rule 3: No loud music at any time.

Rule 4: Swimming pool not to be used by unaccompanied children under 7 years at any time.

Rule 5: No swimming in the pool after 6 pm.

HAVE A GREAT HOLIDAY!

Get started

Copy these sentences carefully and complete them by filling in the gaps using words from the text.

1. Welcome to _____ _____ Holiday Park.

2. May we offer some _____.

3. _____ around the park to get your bearings.

4. Visit our supermarket to _____ _____ with provisions.

5. Enjoy a relaxed holiday, away from the _____ of everyday life!

Try these

Write a sentence to answer each question. One has been done for you.

1. Where can you get more information?

   Answer: *You can get more information at the information centre.*

2. How many pieces of advice are on the leaflet? How many rules are there?

3. Why are there any rules?

4. What do the words 'provisions' and 'unaccompanied' mean? Use a dictionary for help if necessary. What do you think 'hurly-burly' means?

5. Which rules do you think are fair? Why do you think this?

Now try these

1. Imagine you are a visitor to the park. What other information might you want to know? Write notes about questions to ask at the information centre.

2. The information leaflet uses numbered lists. Write one more numbered list for the leaflet. It could tell guests about 'Things to Do' or 'What You Can See'.

3. Think about new ways you could lay out the information you have and design a new leaflet for the holiday park. Perhaps you could draw a labelled map, include a fact file or use a 'Did You Know?' section.

Non-fiction (poster): Fun on Bikes

ANNUAL YOUNG BIKERS' CHAMPIONSHIP

**Crossfield Farm, Westergate
Saturday 25th October**

Juniors (7–10 years) 10.00-12.30
Seniors (11–14 years) 12.30-3.00

(Sorry – no under-7 bikers
allowed to enter)

Entrance fees:
Riders free   Spectators £1.00

Refreshment tent

Get started

Copy these sentences carefully and complete them by filling in the gaps. Find the missing word or words in the text.

1. This poster advertises the Annual _____ _____ Championship.

2. The competition is on _____ 25th October.

3. If you are a rider you can get in for _____.

4. _____ need to pay £1.

5. You must be _____ years old or older to take part.

Try these

Write a sentence to answer each question. One has been done for you.

1. What time do Seniors compete?

   Answer: *Seniors compete from 12.30 to 3.00.*

2. Where is the competition being held?

3. How often does this competition happen?

4. Can you get something to eat or drink?

5. Why do you think under-7 bikers aren't allowed to enter?

Now try these

1. What is the purpose of this poster?

2. What features make this a good poster? What helps the reader?

3. Imagine you went to this event. Write a short diary entry that uses the details from the poster. You could write about what you saw when, what the day was like and what else you did.

Poetry: 'Roger the Dog'

Asleep he wheezes at his ease.
He only wakes to scratch his fleas.

He hogs the fire, he bakes his head
As if he were a loaf of bread.

He's just a sack of snoring dog.
You lug him like a log.

You can roll him with your foot,
He'll stay snoring where he's put.

I take him out for exercise,
He rolls in cowclap up to his eyes.

He will not race, he will not romp,
He saves his strength for gobble and chomp.

He'll work as hard as you could wish
Emptying his dinner dish,

Then flops flat, and digs down deep,
Like a miner, into sleep.

Ted Hughes

Get started

Copy these sentences carefully. They are all lines from the poem. Complete them by filling in the gaps with the words used in the poem.

1. Asleep he _____ at his ease.

2. He bakes his head as if he were a _____ of bread.

3. You _____ him like a log.

4. he _____ _____ romp.

5. He digs down deep, _____, into sleep.

Try these

Write a sentence to answer each question about the poem. One has been done for you.

1. What happens when Roger lies by the fire?

   Answer: *When Roger lies by the fire, he makes sure his head is warm.*

2. In your own words, explain how Roger eats his dinner. Use a dictionary for help if necessary. Which words from the poem are you explaining?

3. Does Roger like to run around? How do you know this?

4. What are Roger's two favourite things to do?

5. What features of Roger make the poet say that he is 'like a log'?

Now try these

1. The words 'like a log' compare Roger to a log. What else could Roger be like? Write down at least three ideas.

2. Find the eight pairs of words in the poem that rhyme. Then write two new pairs of rhyming lines about Roger.

3. Draw a picture of Roger eating or when he is asleep. Use the poem to give you ideas.

Fiction (classic): 'The Tale of Peter Rabbit'

From 'The Tale of Peter Rabbit' by Beatrix Potter

Peter lived with his family in a sand-bank, under the roots of a big fir tree. He was always a problem for his mother, causing trouble and getting into scrapes.

"Now, my dears," said old Mrs Rabbit one morning, "you may go into the fields or down the lane, but don't go into Mr McGregor's garden. Your father had an accident there; he was put into a pie by Mrs McGregor. Now run along and don't get into mischief. I am going out."

Flopsy, Mopsy and Cotton-tail went down the lane to gather blackberries. But Peter, who was very naughty, ran straight away to Mr McGregor's garden and squeezed under the gate!

First he ate some lettuces and some French beans; and then he ate some radishes; and then, feeling rather sick, he went to look for some parsley. But round the end of the cucumber frame, who should he meet but Mr McGregor!

Mr McGregor was on his hands and knees planting out cabbages, but he jumped up and ran after Peter, waving a rake and calling out, "Stop thief!"

Get started

Copy these sentences carefully and complete them by filling in the gaps.

1. Peter lived under the roots of a _____ _____.

2. He was _____ _____ _____ for his mother.

3. "You may go into the fields or down the lane, but don't go into _____ _____ garden."

4. Feeling rather _____, he went to look for some parsley.

5. Mr McGregor was _____ _____ _____ _____ _____ planting out cabbages.

Try these

Write a sentence to answer each question. One has been done for you.

1. Where was Peter allowed to go?

    Answer: *Peter was allowed to go into the fields or down the lane.*

2. Where was Peter not allowed to go?

3. What is old Mrs Rabbit afraid might happen there? Why does she think this?

4. Why do you think Peter went there anyway?

5. How do you think Peter feels now?

Now try these

1. How might old Mrs Rabbit feel if she hears Peter went to Mr McGregor's garden? Write one or two sentences as though old Mrs Rabbit is saying them.

2. Rewrite the story from Mr McGregor's perspective.

3. Draw a picture of Peter in the garden with Mr McGregor.

Fiction (classic): 'The Owl Who Was Afraid of the Dark'

Mother Owl was getting fed up with Plop, a young owl who was afraid of the dark.

From 'The Owl Who Was Afraid of the Dark' by Jill Tomlinson

"Go and find out more about the dark," said his mother. "Ask that little girl down there what she thinks about it."

"What little girl?"

"That little girl sitting down there – the one with the pony-tail."

"Little girls don't have tails."

"This one does. Go on now or you'll miss her."

So Plop shut his eyes, took a deep breath, and fell off his branch. His landing was a little better than usual. He bounced three times and rolled gently towards the little girl's feet.

"Oh, a woolly ball!" cried the little girl.

"Actually, I'm a Barn Owl," said the woolly ball.

"An owl? Are you sure?" she said, putting out a grubby finger and prodding Plop's round fluffy tummy.

"Quite sure," said Plop, backing away and drawing himself up tall.

"Well, there's no need to be huffy," said the little girl. "You bounced. You must expect to be mistaken for a ball if you go bouncing about the place. I've never met an owl before. Do you say 'Tu-wit-a-woo'?"

"No," said Plop, "that's Tawny Owls."

"Oh, you can't be a proper owl then," said the little girl. "Proper owls say 'Tu-wit-a-woo'!"

"I **am** a proper owl!" said Plop, getting very cross. "I am a Barn Owl, and Barn Owls go 'Eeeek' like that. Anyway – you can't be a proper girl. Girls don't have tails. Squirrels have tails, rabbits have tails, mice …"

Get started

Copy these sentences carefully and complete them by filling in the gaps using words from the text.

1. Mother Owl was getting ＿＿＿＿＿＿ ＿＿＿＿＿＿ with Plop.

2. "Little girls don't have ＿＿＿＿＿＿."

3. His ＿＿＿＿＿＿ was a little better than usual.

4. "Actually, I'm a ＿＿＿＿＿＿ ＿＿＿＿＿＿."

5. "I've never met an ＿＿＿＿＿＿ before."

Try these

Write a sentence to answer each question. One has been done for you.

1. What did the little girl think Plop was?

   Answer: *The little girl thought Plop was a fluffy ball.*

2. Why did she think this?

3. Why does Plop think the girl has a tail?

4. Why do you think Plop is cross with the girl? Write as many reasons as you can.

5. Do you think the girl likes Plop? Why do you think this?

Now try these

1. How might Mother Owl feel about the way that Plop's conversation with the girl is going? Write two or three sentences as though Mother Owl is saying them.

2. Think about the little girl's reaction to meeting Plop. Write a short diary as though the little girl is writing it. What might she think about her first meeting with an owl?

3. Draw a picture of Plop speaking with the little girl. Add speech bubbles to show what they are saying.

Non-fiction (information text): Funny Feeders

Fast feeders

Many **frogs** have long tongues. They can shoot them out extremely quickly to catch their food, usually an insect. Then they bring their tongue – and the insect – back into their mouth.

Watching and waiting

Vultures don't kill animals. They circle around waiting for an animal to die, or be killed. Then they swoop down to feed.

Killer plants

Many insects eat plants, but **Venus flytraps** are plants that attack insects! They can close up their leaves to trap an insect. When the insect dies, the Venus flytrap can digest and feed on it.

Plant parasites

Some plants live off other plants. They feed off the other plant without killing it. We call these parasites. **Mistletoe**, which grows in the branches of a tree, is a parasite.

Mosquitoes and some other small creatures, like **fleas**, are also parasites. They live on other animals (including people, sometimes!). They make tiny holes through the skin and suck the blood.

Get started

Copy these sentences carefully and complete them by filling in the gaps using words from the text.

1. Many frogs have long _____.

2. They can _____ _____ _____ extremely quickly.

3. Many insects eat _____.

4. Venus flytraps are plants that _____ _____!

5. Mistletoe, which grows in the branches of a tree, is a _____.

Try these

Write a sentence to answer each question. One has been done for you.

1. How does a Venus flytrap feed on an insect?

   Answer: *Venus flytraps close their leaves to trap flies, which they can then digest.*

2. On what does mistletoe feed?

3. Do vultures kill other animals for food?

4. Do any of the creatures in the extract feed off humans?

5. According to the extract, do all insects feed off plants?

Now try these

1. What is the main point of the information in the extract?

2. In your own words, write three interesting facts about 'Funny Feeders'.

3. Draw a picture of a Venus flytrap with a fly. Label it with information boxes, using the details given in the extract.